SHEL

Ian Patterson taught English for almost twenty years at Queens' College, Cambridge, where he is now a Life Fellow. His academic writing includes *Guernica and Total War* (Profile, 2007) and numerous essays on twentieth-century writers; his translations include Fourier, *The Theory of the Four Movements* (Cambridge University Press, 1996) and Proust, *Finding Time Again* (Penguin, 2004). He has published over a dozen works of poetry, including *Time to Get Here: Selected Poems 1969-2002* (Salt, 2003) and *Marsh Air* (Equipage, 2019). His poem 'The Plenty of Nothing' was awarded the Forward Prize for Best Single Poem in 2017. He lives in Suffolk.

ISBN: 978-1-915079-59-6

Cover designed by Aaron Kent

Edited & Typeset by Aaron Kent

Broken Sleep Books Ltd
Rhydwen
Talgarreg
Ceredigion
SA44 4HB

Broken Sleep Books Ltd
Fair View
St Georges Road
Cornwall
PL26 7YH

Contents

Shell Vestige Disputed

Ian Patterson

Orpheus Says

Kind rules as blind as words see far indeed
and state all traits agreed this form does not yet
model change blown want as leaves assigned
delusion or some version of the real contracted
to require marginal eyes while secret arguments

sustain a way to feel about invisible force to pass
for the sake of bay or nightshade opening
a breach in wonder winding up to vanish or infuse
a deadly Spanish war's image with news of home-made
violent sequels shown on screens in minds each night

more largely bound to overlap cooler turns subtracted
by exchange of reverse tradition no less than a hybrid
verse flower more fully used there as its tension trusting
naked desire to read how margins hold the gate or wait
as vestige of some older wrong, the title lost in weed and rust.

HOME JAMES

Something in the Air

It might be my other image to cling in part that
I owe later to great acclaim with a blue ambition
snare to seize a passage in words of space mirage.

Rapt extremes bitten to speak so at the end of all
the years chances haunted by a nail inward to a list
of anxious benefit and any rarer payee approaching.

But listen, times to his last well straight to what posits
all my signs behind shutters again, invidious idea of
limit shining at each natural hand as signified on this.

Expect invasion in rococo sacrifice proportions, all
white glass and special drift, a treat observed at first
as a mask image of desiring fresh earshot companions.

Had I no answer? I said echo sheds the real word
called intimating matter in debt or believed it all
just off egotism, nobly right since we squared being.

Stake anyone in notice by one pounce in the deep to
clear it up. A loose handle will change your view to
show you how to name ground appeal tucked away alone.

He walked to listen to distance shift in rising attitude
until we bristled with dim elements by the spot of air
known as recital. In short my imagination snapped.

Chance absence led scarce space apart in the air to
travel by lure or menace fitted to her credit guilty of
a mute encounter before lunch for her larger order.

Her front pretext is glad to keep things in the tone
to assuage contrived panataloon fun, forced to meet
a particular affect she ignores by seeing fears get out.

Interest on my side hesitated by a snap of minutes
to draw the world, weigh the trees to the useful class,
talk from the house through a notion wound up to wax.

A flag of light turned actual rupture, a scrap of art noted
till I rest, watch stopped, need on the terrace exposed
conditions clutched in different silent work in language.

Say taste dropped the last birds in the grey wood
pausing in prowl or stalking the approach as if a picture
of a secret lantern before a sponge to keep clear now.

Nothing Doing

Yet lucidity was lost in avenues by the lapse of
a margin to vibrate my last remark so my mind at
the end of an odd memory dropped field gestures
up my deeper sleeve. And there was nothing in it.

My own free straws moved in refuge with a shade
quite yet as a change by law to form old presence
and drop a minute watching a long revolution lost
in so chill a taste I wanted to recall the juncture of it.

I asked why a grip results in proof in space, deepest
matter over baffled scruples full of refuge state in
smoking shadow. I asked too much of the instinct
a formless touch in a wave of velvet gloom sacrifice.

There was something of a time step before we could go
by the smoke abyss dropped in paint, my right to private
wonder, my step a trifle apart, equal to that in another ear
for keeping room to turn away with no chance lost.

It was stupefying. A desert displaced on the spot
with a click and spread to a single wreath over rash flight
without leakage was sure to serve bad work or strike
back in her hand. Who needed this vast memory to speak?

Twisting night can be against sacrifice by putting up
a house of cards. It all exhaled a question. Tell me my tone
when a whole hand of personal state seems still a reason
for taking nothing to gain in a corner of your crisis.

Recollect my state for more news from dead delusion
with instant speculation and candid words to act under
in another place, a leap full of fools gone wrong, spectacle
held in a fictive exchange by the inner liberty of feeling.

Peculiar Pertinence

Nothing lasted to say inevitable in a flash. Collapsed once
for the account, my levity ventured all they don't embroider
to do justice in the act of horrors like strong eyes in his state
of thought. Vagueness was really the whole air, deep trifle.

Question this thought in breath pressed hard about the spot
with deep care, an instant to rub my spell without a lie to still
nobody left. More to save than my system, your logic, my
darkness, on the free note of time and its form being cast.

Revulsion deprives the odd ground gaping with inward echo,
to effect matter now and lift a case to bed in patience. Down
for an instant in a glass and granite look while a fresh shadow
was fitted along the ruins, my figure watching their order again.

Pile hands now as if it was not too late for your stupid idea,
see water before you imagine matter as anything of value to
shake from the moment's scent of dust, a pinch of your time
to match a question of a place gouged out and left, not to have.

Look at the word and then sort it by light and weight, sharp as
logic, as flint, as sound itself in minute touch of the present
array gathered to smash the weight of years of my own, sense
left without sound, the last word done to prompt escape of tone.

Planted Presence

Felt matters these living in the grave of his fears,
a help to an alien, a lateral flame of present air
by the general state in a year or two of climates.

End the rest by a step to avert scruple to call that
element a mind left in the light of analogy found
still in the habit of darkness and sleet on her nerves.

Damage touch accruing, obscurity of matter might
stretch amends as burst vision nursed in silence
to pass by the risk imputed to wound and defeat.

You might confess to pirates, know my finger, show
words in action choked out of a book. Dry it, shrivel it!
Any fool does know you dream of gaping interest.

Pull a shapeless object up a wall bound to the last
time of her strange name as a balm for a price of pity
worse than to drop away the minute it offers hope.

To make up lost fear and expose the knife in case
spoiled chance jerked to renounce an idea of cruel
justice, an aid to the first word for possible even.

Why should we dream of cards on his side, cleft for me?
I offer time as theory to use as a nutshell, to remain
to strike lucid matter in another flaw by actual attitude.

Implacable Grasp

Fortress trash after a blow to live up to as if
instructed for old eyes by venture where things
work to his rose array illusion as to his face .

No bridge after this break or wince if I can do
a miracle count meaning time without desire
then to remember the door, a last light safe.

The street took all sense but he didn't pass the
end so much as gain consciousness of a question
reflected such as to step on another state he found.

Time on the spot would connect the object matter
in a letter so far as the question was back, studied
and cold, each closer day dreamed as apprehension.

No home could be this ground of death free of
voices in a chapter to mark a material fact like fresh
illusions at its feast of air in a word of poetry value.

Short glow fallen to its property of injustice nearer
the word 'stake' and a less silent message beyond a
single part of the face on this ground lived as a chain.

A desire for an order, new vision, a modern threshold
of disgust. To have to dream was the time to enter
the day he never counted the desire of time drinking them.

Nearly Stopped

No scale in the eye of actual intent to get back a word
about ghosts of commerce as secret bounty indebted to
books had even a still winter law person to clear up. Less
in view for so few night-persons as not to have income,
a fancy house, a street-lamp into his dusky eyes for the depth
he was to have to hide in his dream for an increase in time
to settle given excess in hours, or to regard it as language
missing the day at once. Go so far so wet, be a time subject
in renewal, in other words be constituted by a sacrifice scale.
So new to reckon imaging of traceable connections never
let be at this last bargain in place, signs of length falling into
a wish to better the inner voices, his vision of the rooms of
his mind organising to waste time with an idea of his own.
The interest in his queer hand throbs in places dusty and
incalculable, meant to settle his special gasp. A day glimpse
waits behind the vast night, letters dropped into fire, a nearly
blue sense of art mistake, memory of latent space by the door.

Lapsed Step

Artless space had to start a world to remain shut up in
    after the impression by mere point as easiest breath
        a cold square frame, no window, distant light.

Air as element laid bare past service, dropped straight
    from a kind time, missing turns in a deeper care as
        time sank in price tables despoiled without the aid of style.

Brush shadows into shapes like iron and oak, held moments
    saved in so far as they suggest sparse render in lived wrong things
        a tongue above all matters to test as it happened.

Hover with the cup to dose back all the dips that might be
    figured as moments a seam over the view to resolution
        so what was his mind stood new without the nerve.

Heard for instant tap of certain words to live in being less
    alike, less painted, just art going to the verge of ferment
        As the occasion watched for was at once quite affected.

This out of scale character had been sense let into distance
    windows to face a painted figure, air from time settling on
        motive refusal, the first thread of the age, nothing afflicted.

It was best within the frame of eyes turning exposed to dusk
    pain on the wall, a lost face credible to hide, scant marks in
        this dark view of desire. Time could only last under complete vision.

More Measure

Force ease to assist at chill suggestion of a world
of dark escape, pull living air to smoke, sort by ring
tone as fancy nimbus at the eye, quiet fashion by
any case in one of the windows by night and fire
light square for a prowl for final human company.

The key to knowing action now would be chatter
made up to reckon without time striking alone in the
flame of this doubt candle, this minute, this trivial
insistence of light in a crisis, half emerged round the end
of March at windows by the level his eyes lashed at.

Morning exposure going out as if open, the inner
instant catching itself in the doorway of dream life
descent upon self-recognition, head stranger than felt
to be so beyond sense as his own upshot. The idea
divided a present shred, a poor vegetable diet after all.

Some felt form should know some person dropped
the key back to life for time on the occasion as might
any person elsewhere without action of his own. It
was kind of on the spot, difficult to mention later, tones
aware of marks up his sleeve found as secret to the brim.

Least Ground

Nipped off it may be as gage of protection
a margin turned back for the issue of matter
(is it my own shape at the same time of doubt
all being scarce and losing it through the window?)

The grave was blank, time ceased to be solid for
less to exist as strange impressions of the gravity
in me: you can catch his voice by his sense of the future
through this time of given wonder in his tone.

Words trip them ridden by chance for more able
space at the door in this rain as it strikes down
pleasure in case this idea mixed less in that with
all you want to be inferred from a charge kept in.

Further stress delay and any door closed a little to
lurk after being through ground for all the world
to go on. He had to count each strike for provision,
able lungs, a fresh chill later reduced to proof of speech.

Whatever felt strong was pulled up to keep it dangling
in the least mind to think of, something like words for
motion, and leave by the grave of doubt over the world
waiting far below. Come to the door and plunge in wrong.

Flagrant Number

The effect of lack heralded in a general sense of coin repeating
his flagrant things, his way of meaning disclosed all round some
inward manner, time bent to clear or press the spring and wait

not even an hour in a rattle of recall, so he heard himself felt, indeed
wasn't he only air and windows, emptier than the sea? Matter was
swallowed up near windows, raised at sight of work as it all might be.

Right relation nick the gasp of suddenness, make wings of going
with breath on force into the room. No stranger leap, his feet felt need
going, they said, above fact, so press air into any lapse of a moment,

air and so time as frame after the fact quite without casting back at
the plunge as figure of a father. Brush escape flood died under the
whole page, stirred air to the instant. Repetition of being heard even.

Least Ignorance

A hung cause fell under matter for blood put to show
to be all recital of the house story, kept at last as guilt
put up in every civil name, enlarging a posture lapse.
Such a virtue flourish in any ground itself might rate a legend
as the swell of vision, as the next turn, as a full subject,
as even a purpose for his grasp of a handle broken off.

On your side, you gasp, they tell me, with blows patched
astray for a sight of difference and a signal of best scruple,
the only thing to like. I told about the wonder in time to
act it, left in miniature words, hard space of lips that fail
at each menace of elapsing artist flight, the gesture dropped
for the moment, the object seeking notice instead of beauty.

That instant remembered now in the secret tip, a hurry to
need nothing still might hang over a minute, close air to
refresh his hate of covers. Any test content ignored in
flushing tacit speech steps out of the article, with a lack of
level hands to humour me. Pocket impressions in edge words
swept away to take up matter to image what I want to say.

Make me care for tone trouble, the all round slip on scarce
distance, each space unspeakable, measured by charge that
both falls and cuts the act by presence denoted as close order.
Plunged in the chill passage with time for a rash effect of
words he had never heard, speech laid by in an inward gasp,
it came as an apparition, a lost tone in his ear spoke dream echoes.

In fact air at that pitch disposed in dark looseness might take
back all prime matter. Less time for world presence in that part
of the vagueness, so extend this figure and stroke memory of
the glimpse and act with style. Stamp under the rush to seek a
minute of full arrival. Nothing joined, sealed or fitted wings to
him. How had this voice just made his ear hold that sort of reserve?

Clear Nothing

Pulled up before a form of honest person, all come
    to gape for profit fixed on signs of brute air on ground
        matter, a strain to make up the fold of surface breathing

To go out of being grasped, while he felt nothing for the time
    clothed and lapsing at a stroke of the door. Desire to this effect
        first fell on faint justice in the failure open to him to inspire.

He had dreamed of breath. A sacrifice of eye grace so manifest
    in a case of absolute alarm, windows bolted for this neat unknown
        at hand with a dull presence of material you couldn't begin to

represent or want such vibrated sense of measure. A flash of
    advance by real ceremony, the end minute was to be the least
        mark of stupid comfort, the force of being voiced and ordered.

Tight Orbits

Silly desire for instant stress care pushed the will past any
ground of his feet so the word might be only measure
or manner formed like sense rising in arms and legs by resort
to vision, staring up his sleeve, to appeal for company as
shade breath on impressions of motion.

His words seemed to span your head trouble, still turned
back for quite due caution of addresss, the best spot on the
host body for form to invite a glimmer of wanting to be
intent on finding hard tact in speaking eye time if you care
more than nothing, mired in time to eat.

Say nothing apt to free a mite of frolic, a little left freshness
afraid of thought, in fear of power despite his figure of doubt.
Waiting must clearly do more to weigh things when the vexed
minute is a sense impulse letting it recognise an instant as
queer movement complication quite at ease.

Interfering time proved instant desire hindrance, a glimmer
to watch in air afterwards as well as to pick the same time
in any occasion to counter the other way in. Usher or
foreshadow power again by the tone as first despatched, sure
to share in words before time and intention.

Don't say I want out of the quick air of perception. Sense
happened to have to seem salient, showing vision losing
the stroke to act betrayal by tacit delay at home. Drudge at a
distance fit to toast the style of pain by the visit, making a
boast in time to mind the body to matter.

Patch over feet in time, save the present show to breathe
instant means in the measure of chill felt from talking about
being minded to figure a body lurking and wanting in time
by the nick of fear. Renewal of vision, the house in the lapse
already out with why the world looked ill.

Point instant fresh and own the rest to bear. Laugh to
see when to take another guess at time, answer free at once
in vital doubt of the same stroke of her eyes, inclined to
doubt dream abuse, this moment and time and sense and
no effect to intend a conscious want to touch.

Provoke Better

Look sure for where he was and how it was in the eyes
nature had liked better, even for the minute. The house
might grow measured, a space apart against manner or
form in a glance at a shock he minded, confused for the time
as a wish to remember the matter of a laugh, wanting to
crop any instant harder. Stupid speech interest went on
to take in events by impulse as much as what you call captive
remark, in such things as eyes, matters he grasped away
in order of writing. Come to the window and suppose a
fresh mine of instant show to pocket the secret box, missing
with a certain pinch. His need to doubt every quiet inspiration
was now just passages with light on a slight letter protest
with art fashion success moment, the taste for matter
remembered in grace. The lapse admitted light renewals
to the room: it was before the pages haunted over this fact,
pen to the ear in right fusion from terms of further effect
denied later desire. Know the window as if in a play in your
absence, always to lose heart whenever you look over the
letter you lost and need, only an instant to ignore the taste
of restless time, not to avoid the act of direct flight from
art, wanting the troubled look as a sign to shut your eyes.

Defeated Scale

Drop weight while facing the breath of practice reflected
          in tone less possible with the presence of
heavy reply saying so. It permitted nothing that would affect
          another world in this scarce snuffle any more
than a dream as light as need and control in fresh tribute to
          judge moments beyond the bristle of a step
to your eye distance for all time, to wink between the impulse
          and the matter in proportion to his figure of
the grasp of force, muffled or loose as the question of his
          words passing the window, silent and set to carry on.

Dark Otherwise

Miss the account more civil for performed need
to leave credit, the utmost return to benefit in this
hand of information time checked with a language
to speak into my head. Even a minute bore the
worst look observed so that my name fits this
shrinking field of vision talked about as doubt or
virtue. Too much is quite enough, you wish to claim
work as disappointed rest, steps as some degree mine
to fall back on, a home for nothing less than gravity.

Miss the name of flush probability, miss right saying
appeal to doubt, but limit agreed matter in declared
lip pleasure, scarcely begun for wholly sharp relief
of circumstance. That instant force would be
apprehension, impatience for the moment to show
where I ought to desire to feel cut off in other words
for the absurd question of secret humiliation there
in a word uttered in the light, the answer to things
pledged to the old order, having to breathe so hard.

Doubtless Matter

Apart still among the art of blankness with names for
a word to express being like nobody obliged to miss some
other creature then blaze out in time in the dreadful room,

trust your sudden effect more than that supreme exchange
of the impression of a force to oppose for a reason, look for
the key on a broken patch of much more than my words ask for.

I break with looking for the expected, at least as I have to let it hover
in a shade cast for a moment in its face, hide in air to recover
from that occasion to be the question I surprise as an image door.

To push open, I mean. Admire or follow, I am in the room.
Look at the end of time, beyond free speaking, spare that long
matter for a kind of threshold when I hold together and know that.

His fingers threw light into a justice interval to measure failure,
reading his speech rupture as some imitation of the crisis, his
care annihilated to chill dismay of stone, a drop of mortal instant.

The suspense thus attested seemed a hand at the door before
calling again for the pleasure of the last fancy years ago, eyes
as words in the mind, in fact pronounced as a glance of information.

The entrance, the stair: all made up in exchange, detached from
any step to the window with nature noted at the time by betrayal.
Some sense of right words for your cross ears, that was the tone.

The candid spasm of explanation here interposed as a sudden
response to personal discipline was to pile up her cell-effect
rigours to the open door to your time, never so much wanted.

Moments of constriction caught him in the act of inspiration,
a word trifle tightened by sharp spot warrant, without other tribute
to render about the turn in your house, letting that figure choose.

Strong Original

Felt ruffle for quickness, the air taken from his world,
    his mouth repeated sharpness as liberal array expression
        at once denied even tragedy now, art supported by small matter,
    the slope by his match open to bristle understanding how
this bridge to others' hands was altogether behind his back.
    To flare apart a sign or blow breath in quick promise was
        the site of an imagined voice applied with confidence at a
    scene retention, a violation of the ear, unconscious in that
element felt in time with some organ, a shade of great words
    that might continue telling parts of him to come out
        as the phrase to glint and gather alarm deprived of action.

Impute impressions of relation to turn to the door, sense
    before asking for your eye to judge almost a page even
        to call most thought of hope to flower for credit time
by private instants, not many, drawn from want of other
light resources to put it in the sea by accident, hope warning
    as chill promise suspended. In fact shadow appearance as a
        step might touch awareness and measure the original reading.
    Aim to just desire it as instinct of surrender to any air, still and
flagrant by presence, grin and be a momentary present by this
    time without her occult cause of corrected fancy through the
        strange stress this worst was the author of, held as caring.

Bedevilled Terms

Grasp that moment, signal nothing for that light figure
and give a shade as a place free of vision, no pencil to note
or finish collections of neat caprice as soon as taste a fig or
mark your mind while I speak as I say, being so on the spot.

Where consciousness did grow up to the outer state, crude
symptom of some note of observation given for the fact of
exposure, these pressed each recognition of what surged up
as apprehension as if pursued by that glare, a disguise reflected.

A gasp for weight, transparent spots blur the light, walls in
the dark reach things and pinch matter even to face the idea
of balance, poor spark to complain of spirit shade and piece
words from the ground, the object world of broken touch.

Making that up, all names strike me as determined to be at
liberty with a hint of content desire moving to the sound of
parts of perception, scaring arrival in this grasp for an idea of
explaining a moment watching light flicker on wings again.

Actual Selection

Take ten more to temper identification, use the name
of a house now the set penalties turn violent. So much left
to say the part after minding more than saying words
his mouth uttered, in a sense believing whatever words
were spoken before the public. That strange motive just
measured the moment, lost touch as words waiting for
people with an object, a sort of justice to believe in, as
eyes fail to think for the mind in the dark blue time that
grew, as his hand for an instant imputed to the sharpest
instant an expectation, watching. Wait and let it come,
tell me the place, darker and branching. Figure it out.
How had he said such waves of recall, left that word quite
as matter with a still reflection of these moments,
their searching light less attested and unexplained already.

Whirled Attention

Reach through the question uttered without
moving to touch the wound seen by nothing
less than strange pressure from speaking it, as
the final twist between the house and the day

Matter into view, mutely next to this gift caught
close to tight mutual glare after the back of the
exchange measure. But eyes with anxiety, the
effect of words, mean to end moments of it all

The object in his sight has to glimmer at me
to affect you, catching it worse than free talk,
a bit afraid to be wishing to see friends in the
shade, dangling in the air, tracing the far range

Such a stir of suspicion, a plastic perch grasped
without moving in order to visit the house by speech
to the ear. You'd like the country, to leave there
tired of pretending to return the air in confidence

I come back from nothing down to a mention
in instant witness by blind pressure of doubt,
the rest of time even here for my own present
shadow, for the air I had taken for granted

Spot cast in light reflected in the known effect
blinked at a lost place in the world, in the room,
in the stress of being portended as if touch left
the very things we had shaken off repeated times.

Impression Really

The trouble at the moment was not for the world
hurt, a dim drawing in instant thought like fear in
what he'd suffer in his answer to the idea of form,
but a second look out of the light of scrap earth we
all love. Don't change this show of touch, this figure
of dropped care in the tone of words as various desires
needed in order to arrange a common ground for
each to risk. Time to get more time wound up, wanting
to live half-prepared to agree more and be sad about
this growth of word trouble, renewed blankness as
the question of the break in the form of pitch and sound
in moments that glow to apprehend no answer to
brush away in knowing advantage, as he would.

Peep Contact

Quickly as I told you the world let alone at last
seems to warn you to forswear your effort to act
upon wound up breath of inevitable forces and
carry off understanding in your hands, as if shade
was all edges for a moment, a prickly presence to fix
an instant with formless sound, unseen sense of
time struck silent. No one departed out of the
door, the open look at something that drove it in
by the ample house quitted by eyes and some sound.
Words without attention to the door at last addressed
the tone of renewed doubt, signs of measure as lack
of nearly nothing; the issue is thought in light and
proportion about conscious hours repeated as
perversity again, passing sharply after an instant
exposed to fear, to flutter more than his lips could tell.
Each well-kept approach would help free our exchange
of touch and find the world ready in divided awkwardness.

Earlier Pocket

Quickly verified possession failed fingers or whatever
shone without mine. How he held a mode of bright
instant, a bovine air of physical breath, still drew
the glare of contained eyes, another object, back to
the door. The effect of his face hung on spoken views
soundless for a time after the first jostle. Mute as to
beg to make him appear at a sign intended to measure,
wound up for something. Now this to reflect on presence
and hours to swallow up in another sense. Aware of the
rest, perhaps information after you see expressions like
want and believe at a pitch that turned like touch in
words—in their echo, he meant. If air was concentrated
measure as a contrast to set in the house before we
choose light, the idea might have been aware of the
different recall haunted by conscious strain, a long time
to be denied comfort and certitude. Most without being
aware of a figure of imagination So few instants to match
strange people. So you fail to discern the other note, the
future of measure, the past of sense accumulations and
continuities in time. At least add show as bewilderment
meeting trouble as recent time unexpectedly hurt in its
function, as if the same question was drawn to play off
breath quite beyond light. Conceive any matter as a sort
of injury appeal. Air felt still. Other things would be said,
be published as an idea in time beyond any power of sense.

Sense According

A postscript

A short street to get to material occupation, the door I groped for many years ago. Time before that account wanted to believe in the surface of my show, my final distress months' duration.

I dream or mean to be avoided in the process of this strange exhibition. Vividly to own all that interval lost in the past, saved in fear as the substance of waste words here. Uncanny desire.

Facts conceal it, material like consciousness of this question in circles arranged in air in glimmers of economies of sense. I just nail things to catch this dictation, an accident floats in my head.

The moment taken over to this wavering margin to speak of living in this sense of divination, to own the ground portent, work the world loose from the air in the house, sprawl in the evoked aspect,

Come near the matter in tone. What I want is to grasp each nail by betrayal of the terms of catastrophe, collapsing the ground in this modern measure. It may help to keep the question in so many words.

My free hand requires pages of flesh, a kind of literal mind. Nothing extracted in a message to you, resting eyes on the house as the balance between two to speak a word of what I mean not to say, a note in advance.

A SPACE BASED ON HEARSAY

Air Flitter

Binding light over the brow thrown from the air soft
matter incapable of rhetoric assuming status attention,
with so true an eye to extract value out of our reach, why
mean to explain such posh dismal magic as fictional wish?

Fly over the wall wearing a show made good in another
language, press a petal to rags to doubt about moving out
of time as a scene offers to flutter the tongue and grove
and flood the whole array with pastoral multiplex parody.

Begin inset reason of shadow rakes to recognize the
moulded conflict he or she brings by the yard to music. It
is not necessary to explain four words as a form left behind
in a seclusion that works with silence or an Aeolian harp.

Abiding in their back yard containing the words called art
of losing, it's still there in the sense of a glimmer impulse line
cut back at the end, as burnt lists shake against the cold mind
on implied stress, like a mouth blight still without rhythm.

Stuck material points well up and go back as what follows
from an email dream first without shouting so much in bed.
Time on concrete sift to brief air ruin. Notice a message as it
stands for everyday models of relief in the mouth or body.

Spice this object in abject damage space to a yard of void sense
marked out in unhinged tenses, a way to consume that thought
understood as a sight no longer missing an origin sensed about
the wings of matter as they fade over and over into air flitter.

Gloomy Clamber

Exotic narrative city to malign each day permitted stop and
search side street caginess or brim aware through the gates
least aperture soon told while strolling back all fearful for flight
steps back down midsummer ratchet shift for some ancestral
theory of struggle. Dog remedy fails under the sun, falls again.
Zoom contact page scroll, chestnuts and acacias a partial
antidote outside this approach to plain stories or lives. String
out getting shot of it all, alley between variables endemic to
wider issues, cycling beside the canal. Repose in the letter, money
to efface the destructive movement a mere abstraction. Stop-
gaps concede a cloud of oblivion in common time, walkable
traces leading to emergence of fingertip dislike, even hate. To
what purpose all this bird twitter chat scrabble in bramble
tangle nobody can say, throats constrict at the thought of such
lucidity, bare as poles as far from innocent we glance at black maps,
all inert, s-shaped and unconsulted in this feverish puzzle.

Exceed Frame Time

Greeting studded internet predictions
burst through glint, left now only like
sun squalls, with core time building up
on the edge bent a little defaulted to
late snow on the sea, up from the drone.
My first number shrug happened too
far out to deal with, say a car left
by the quarry for a voice call, take charge
of some ancient bucket, look away or
strain fate by crane to another place.

Plate glass closure, savage tray put down,
no rubber bands, no screwdrivers, a copy
of the spirit, some flying creature at last
filling part of the air, lost to sight. Numb
race to violent counter answer explicit and
essential fittingly. Not failed, comrades,
save the material world, the chest freezer
heritage boutique guilt store. Rinsed under
clouds, touch flaking to reveal an absence
of what was imagined as assemblages.

That nail connects light to bramble, keeps
anxiety cobbled to one hand, a field of
force full of density if you squint a bit
to mint focus adjusted for hawthorns and
ash. Hinge tremors return unsaid each night
begun in speeded-up promises, just you
wait and see. Least shed, pelt freely. Hear
today this morbid outcome broadcast,
rain forecast to slope in between scales
taken up quite cold and not itself shared ever.

Get an Ear Test

Guess with submerged forms to attend
to, note some goal constructs in the concept
here supplied with time off limits to turn
clear back. Each look for later hover
flies, raked lavender, told about it, known
to be false as a kind of opposite to need
the earliest threat to earth you remember,
now all this and its dead eyes lurking as a
special undergrowth offer you can't refuse
or know about, perky intrusive hazels. Get
over here, feign colour for foreign shapes,
think licorice touches recombined in sphere
manifolds no questions asked. Thistle and
goat's beard allow a pause. So call it music.

Potentially Permanent

Parallels speak further things, the weather itself
to give support status leaks over high ground in
this wider sense, action or reading as an opaque
fabric, a veil against any ephemeral perception.

Total balance averse, muffle decoys conspire to
never end or stumble as one might too easily yet
carry on to doubt embodied plunges, safe from
this rough story as it falls in words that flap about.

Who needs subject form in closed aspect or in a
wider memory process usually well filled by rakish
nature enduring distant interests, no plot winding
a puppet fantasy of public life in draft wish code?

Just hand the desire and fill out the normal case
present tense state, cloud ahead and visions inscribed
from green pages in the mouth. A title word hangs
unspoken, a circling buzzard its bogus parallel.

Oh no, no buffer grinding. Earth heave butterfly
fear, bottle tremor translated to the clouds as innuendo,
spreading shadow to remain a lot of stuff, words
crammed in the photograph crawling like repro ants.

Yellowhammer rustle in the flash ear, carbon lost out
in the air, vagrant beings the mock shadow stretches
like a manifesto focus grin across the grass all aflutter,
a poor bubble of the inner self we never close now.

Please Call Us

Knot some broken focus quite up tight
as bees rise and fall by the dream outfall,
unable to be marked as frank attention to
an imprint secretly with a pollen ring
panic regarding some tumult of sublime
memorial shining over voices muttering
behind fountains. Stillness leaves.

It left, civic pride left in a way that reused that
frame, this web, to set more air into the space
above literal sense in years to come, to puff
up custodians of ordinary personal problems
and manage further discourse for cash. Grass
matted, autumn crocus glowing at the edge
half-grasped thoughts shaped by waking.

The ring panic never left, sea-level clout dis-
placement amounting in practice to an island
of waste in a sea of waste. Nobody answers
the hunger tangle calling by day in choked
shivers of warp enigma. A sort of quietness
arrives like menace or footsteps and stays.

Why Call it Again?

It went against the glass, anything but
compressed life face to the green ones
lacking a far cooler origin, with intended
motifs as rapturous machine objects. We
invent chaotic bias in order to see the
contours' maximum energy impacted—
or worse, not afraid of the past, abstract
and close to lyrical incessant gusto. There's
no reason to call it anything else now, just
call it by its name. Its name against yours,
filmy hopes message syndrome spot cash
reality drawn to owl noises through the
darkness, what more can I say? Almost
placid again, reflect on it, reflect it back.

Only Displacement

Supposed to possess drafts for when I started
those neglected words about what visual trial
might last a life in the version cut for time, a
few chosen sentences in an array of radiant
tumult, enough to compose an oblique speed
present, scraped away, seeing things dying, what
urban beings keep in mind as ambiguity, it might
be in order to point a brief new shaping fiction.

Cue sparks, closed footpaths, assumed creed
departed as rain falls steadily over the abyme, a
cascade some time ago seeded to seem now not
remembered, immune to habitat missing the light
to boost each lurch to name text's spurious smile,
eroding slowly to act as a type of abandoned gradient
by sad experience wise and fluttering diction
speaking honey near hope to filaments imparted.

This was imagined. Or at least an attempt to read
through the fissures of a voice to get behind the dial
and into the works, to see how there might be arcadian
observations in sudden flights above the trees, friction
between concepts, black versions nestling towards night
and the barn-owl sailing towards me. Always a climb, a
dying ash back by that hedge, hips and sloes got
in heavy weather up there to wet the lake as birds darted.

Some kind of fiction then. Clouded air for a while
puffing thought stuff into old frames, like the tradition
of dead generations caressing the eye and backing in fright
from the daylight as woods decay and call faint-hearted
feeble cries to the slipshod act of model camera shot.
All go on ruined each from far to sell from hand to crime, a
loss to us alas in adverts for the last chapters, with obedient
elders smiling in deleted expectation of a right to need.

Past Taste

Respond by larks hum kindly light
       tasting of dropped vanilla in a hybrid
field placed to one side fixed into this
       attempt to reveal communal minds
to describe really ignorant bubbles
       of each perception to surmount
a stroll through the forest within
       as for instance friends clearing
access to concept functions and points
       that would be free and unbounded
approaches to vision enfolded in
       radio waves in spite of space rashly
kind woven through lasting signs
       unsounding between each and
over e.g. a cat mutual-hearing humans
       from windows posed to provide
instance in essential vision charting
       complex far experience manifest
and nettled by unseen bunting chats
       once lost from memory as proper
calls reply from twig rebates and must
       deepen to remain caught in time

Leaving No Trace

This spiral prank a collared dove's slight twitch
lost a last twig now hold fast a challenge in hand
to calibrate brash earth so easily lost to pointless
fiction permanent hurt twizzle uncaptured daily

Writers blind as possible disabuse in language
behind the voice solid sound opening to cliché
moments of partial meat around lace obsession
over wallpaper stubs that appear back at the tether

Of wood-tongue slipway refusal long in reverse
even so, and recently driven off that piece of land
leaving what goes real to speak of paradise or
some woodland grudge posture claiming the right

To it. Little meaning of their own dogs what they
think they say, disarray in the ear if it fails to cosset
our long wake sense as after supper defiance breath
shapes what leaves nothing but a footprint everywhere

Of Denser Things

It was the latch to an extent not shadowed now
      gelid light valley leaves moss and lichen reticent
a ravenous montage echo ritual, food for pattern
      recognition software in hands growing up against
parallel future circumstance caved in for partial
      smudged windows down two points on human life.
Left out stacks observe banded material walls
      wood strips imagined desires the implausible view
bound in compass flash full screen tongs as if only
      current hopeful appetite would shun such solidity,
a norm-busting moment of death-watch artery in
      vetiver image translation reproachful. Gasp impulse
radical to gnarled film gesticulation memory shivering
      then suffering made up of tracts of threat thread
to shift what satisfaction might engorge the present day
      after day, its steamy edges blue sticky and intolerable.

TO ACCOUNT FOR

About The Dark

Controversial as for an innocent and open
miscarriage of speed as sound as less or all
we could explain, why it had to work on the
volume loan story of his plan with his vast
cost, ardent readers or any trick on his own
charge source; and his account is different
to give it clear notes falling to help treat all
the echo context. All apart springs solid law
tasked to pain material speech, any books
to a rise in the language of appetite to life
between two deaths pronounced and over
written as nobody has ever done it before,
books of unimaginable size but no meat in.
This is the dark. Part of ordinary workings
because of night or the cage while it lasts.

Look at Them

Glimpse twisted look back struck expression
burning apparition silent unreality unwinding
a late doubling apart from time in the letter as
weeks run on eating the future today, vacant
last dream abandoned all odder reason to
dread each flat trace to occasions knocking to
improbable standard silence. Waiting bravado
shadows glared with quartz bell expression of
hands as intruders prepare to speak, confused
calm sigh to go back to even happen better by
acorn movement ignored, forced into being,
those on the edge burning where they must stay
in part gutted by the roots of quiet let far in the
trees falling flutter space cut by white sky over
my eyes, rigid obsession to care to come up this
uneasy hour to talk one way when I had heard.

Consolidated Uproar

The security exception text measure or crisis
in perfect times of domestic debt purchase,
requiem chair not yet grasped as we only now
dismantle this drain rebound epidemic behind
the counter backed through language-networks
insult, my whole account loss is to be swindled
by fertile grounds for dormant set allocation in
nesty hedges singing like nightingales in the
dust, well I ask you. A call is specified and
not in use. Strain is a secret looking about the
problems I got to know, a wryneck in ivy hardly
seen let alone heard above all this clatter reset
as separation from silent musing a few years later.

Inlaid Reflection

What noise supposes reason nod towards
shoulders in the past few weeks to pause
again by the letter pool, escape very near
wanted actions in the street to divide and
want others saddled between a time of this
or that, liability being when past returns to
begin here in my life mostly among ash trees.
Frogs disappear for shame if not against
reverberations, by some tug from stone
terror jarred again at dawn, all in motion's
embrace and lines of code hurrying back
to hail the body effect, footprint in mud,
slap as it darts away from the register and
off the record. Now inhale all the fragments.

Just Thermal Slash

Hot days review ramps without some forbidden fern
refutation close to hand, nothing to lament. Leaves
if you say so all away from the bank like snow, like a line
surging on words for my brief turn early one morning
just in a flash impression to keep broken in the dirt,
always yours empirically or very well may serve to break
the ice as goldfinches do. Lucid strain, a table in need
of chance gift scales, poetry for economists with a word
about time by the window to empty lattice arrival of
the fittest, curious to the question edge, now completely
consumed. Splutter away, too good to be ivy, too old
for voices spilling rage as dry leaves temper a ground,
boots in the dark at the same time plainly heavy with
a need to know. Owls may be sheer expanse of air by
the field, not much choice, even wonder against hope.

Faint Last Abandon

Turned open on dead wind consequence to
walk down to the better house in a way not
less than I could follow by ear, by switch access
to deal with land broken uniquely. Wait to
speak time to power, breathe to stone, hold
it in mind, mark wire shock wrong at the end
or wave and drift as you would say at my wit's
end. Wit's end weddings. Hark, hark, the lark
in another world. Right up against stone, cold
presides, held back to yield whatever's left of
treacle or dust or abstract line that hangs about
bracingly unused with rocks and stones and
damp ideas of spirit music. Do what you can.

Intuition Rush

Thunder ruffle tip down sleek leaf shadow,
just another blackbird singing bits of rusty
air, slip to jump up still warm at the bridge
I mention now in front, now forgotten,
only to recur as it surely will under the sway
of fonts in fragments lost, particles clasped
to echo watery prints of appropriation
that make me gasp in pale strips of breath
quickly known before traces of feeling
sink back at the outfall. Abandon hope all
moving things snaffled equably in a sort of
moral balance attack on network sites. Slight
ruins quake to rid the world of all it contains.

Allowance to Hand

Another time abated, ages left for me,
left to my choice regret as long as talk
felt by display to occupy or deprive fret-
ful manners, paid language gloom always
more anxious and under-theorised in a
part detritus filter, part citric thought
pattern of long shed struggles writ large.
State of change, herbal profusion, bees
bumble and hum in petal tent labour,
act mirror colour shift rain dead, time
of departure noted, new mint label to
print. Foot first twinkle at material text
substrate ready to hand it to me as if
nothing happened against the future
darker gloss on flotsam coating swells.

Coppice Fret Verge

Pose trickles slide thoughts framed askew
down the years nothing adds up as super-
imposed presence all there still and gone
for what it's worth. A desk, a window, a
garden, equally framed. Think stamen or
stumble and stammer to jerk it free, red as
verge poppies, frame cut back in strictures
sharp edge insists on. A kind of farming
since you will anyway invest in clouds if
not clods, voter registration, boundaries
of the self macular or spot-on for so many
thistles and dandelions. Tap it all, turn it
on and see what grows in flat texture field
ground down by worry, gaps alert to call
about bat whispers and other lyric devices.

Overt Ruffle Return

Over at the last air pressure gasp, gaps in everything,
even three at least graven in space as they say to resolve
a discrepancy. Now they fall like apples thud-haunting
each sound dropping slow in grass scythed for the time
as steps promise to slam it all home in lexical antinomy.
Grist spilt over night's doleful train noises, what can it
mean? Tailor's chalk end-stopped, visible shell of thought
going pink pink, social distance among the leaving airs
so sweetly set and graced, guest vision lurking behind
the form to fill in with a handful of earth if you'd do the
rest in peace in your own time please. Do say what you
hear about the ride when you land behind the screen:
plastic system at a loose end, beware slippery surface
curving back through brambles or nettles, odd memories
liable to flood and cause distortion or feed it back.

IMAGINARY SKY

The *Woods*, where *Beasts*, or herded *Men* abide,
As thick are planted *there*, and near their side
Fantastick People too, in *false Fields* move,
And *Fowl*, in larger *Fields* of *Aire* above;
Swift, as the *winged Thought*, that feigns their *flight*,
Yet never *soaring* out of *inward Sight*;
Though with their *fancied Wings*, they higher *flie*,
And traverse all th' *imaginary Sky*.

— Richard Leigh

A Hasty Dip

Half belonging to this regard a hasty dip
may be its final nicest question to do
out the way like a room for the walls
at midsummer, from the first comfort
kept to lose and then you have even
this dry view with the lapse of years.

Darker shades of some head invited
for colour, a fresh alarm pitch for an
elastic interval message, a warning
emphasis right through the first hour
of omission. Turning in a moment
in his private circle, asked to mark it

as apt and weak like an old story
made violently new, all done up to remain
a subject loosely doubtless in measure.
In a fine fact of exposure motive haste
he struck her as sign, as degree, call it
nothing uttered, not even a word subject.

We've just managed to say nothing of
the short wave tension rather lighted up
from China and wired to the line. No
lines conscious of poor scribble for a man
she held exposed to allusion but nothing
was as it was once begun, my finger on the bounds.

So of dreams when traces stab at a figure
I sing. I begin from behind my head
with a blot to trample as my head feeds me
and climbs my stick collage with all the art
in the world exercising obstacles as a child
would have been its customer or eaten it all up.

What Ever Next?

It was about context responsibility first
written in the difficult motif of a class and
signalling at the outset none of its value
had to be axed to document the virus poll.

What were these birds? Lost from vineyards
lost from spindle lost from the map of music
day to day to prompt us depleted to eat
what we hear as silence pleated in the ear

and create islands of smirched glass etching
them instead, scorched years of blasting to
fetch in the last remnants ever told or drilled
to buggery short-term and strictly off the books.

Welcome galanthus glimpses lighten to redeem
what nothing else for it lost to dark or troubled
hand to collar drove wrongs collected red bar to
press or expected proposals pushing up through.

Snow drops from the cloud formula unfurl in
masks as streetwise shingle hives a loud melancholy
raw air played thin on distant wires single sweet
noises dire warnings to range away in order

to continue the soundings beyond mountains.
The detained miles lucent merge in memory
from moth clutter to spam fritter grim pastures
and impostures all lost as remnants of old music are.

Stitch to hamper a blue button, expect to use its
register in wild drugget underfoot meshwork
if only once or twice with eyes fresh and open
wide, ladder back balanced by twigs as if to say

most words deliquesce here in the wood's raw
gains. Barge telepathy less strongly flows to
plug the gap variant trend in material impact
per capita, notably in income, now wide garble.

Where the ever more sublime fumarole gasps
interrupt word thought expressed as pierrot sigh,
what remains of all the salient world so girt
with wrong brash twirling tweets against us?

Look now, a green fireplace addressed as change
trading notes in pleasant components scratched a
kind of theatre of chance in work known to make
chores for thumb or teeth in a lost projected refuge.

In the mid smile switch off a magnetic vocal
fox in casual decades of woodland out of choice
used precarious cheap song panic, some club in a
blind rule category noted all right to darkness.

People call it a wren habit spelling 'foredoomed'
and bent on obsolete classic survival power, far
down by yon bewilderment, aback if you peer
more dimly towards the old place of a morning.

But what other thing follows next was written
only for several days, stirred up the wretched past
of no importance. To meet allusion did one good
and paid no attention to whatever it might have been.

Another Subject Incline

Against a landscape, sleep will convey
doors disputed in excess flow and speak
the place it has to determine or negate.

Image limits can stand ego springs to
arise in never-ending limp plays from the
zone of warmer days obligingly in another

matter of course, in a dismal mask followed
at sense pace in fused edges slipped up
twixt cup and mix-up plunged in our plight.

Stripped down kind of eye sedge puffing
up to incline again for weeping as it leads
to give mind its oily draft surface by the marsh,

inclined to wander claim to slash enlisted
process skein by cloud shapes by skin lucky
sleeping vellum bound to settle a tune.

Or steal one from the tune orchard, panic
rummage too much for a refuge in stupid
heat, a key in a door too much for a voice

to invent or sing to envelope everything
in a cloud of ongoing superfluous sense,
words summoned to contradict all music.

Infernal Duo

Where in all this listed detachment of human
diversity and stake problems is a cause of fear
cloaked by a final offshoot of inverse time? If
the book collapses in so short a period, do they
attend my best mind printed or claim total
fairness? The centre is left out, turned down
from the angle of this war as they did with every
irony in his flat. It became a fashion like the
phonology of wallpaper, a song of salvation
whispered in places apart, evidence even of
resistance to something in the air, nothing to
get hold of except that earworm and a voice
trying to tell you it was scripted to live through
it again and again. Only be told the best, it said.

Radish Nostalgia

Or banish unofficial rose disguise that
blows up time immemorial a gorge to
hanker after. This afternoon my prism
for cloudy climbs, my cover story now
basically rounded with superimposed
marginal teeth in self defence. Half eaten
I dream.
                    Red posters up
at corners I began reading again between
a line not crossed, an eye not doubted
as stonecrop and hawkbit crop and bite
and grow. Jackdaws all day here. Let
them come they will.
                    Profusion atone
and bless each reticule kitchen, tender
refusal fine birth for supper glimpses
ever open utter blending hero reduction!
Might also drips. As night devours the car.
Whose lips are right or often say they are.

Lemon Sole

At first glance the edge sign tempts
to that code below we now find so
fond of so little, nothing about coffee
to go out of date except this danger of
the edge of things so to be overlooked.
Tap fear entry beyond the scope of
this key absent at flowing time don't
you see what I mean, hooked they can
be simple uncomfortable thoughts or
be hand in club twitching under a table
set for three or more. Wood pigeon
trunk calls charred wire woodcut to
fix up and running a sort of ladder to
betterment set with my own hands. Eat.

I'm Not Sure

What critical vice you are told to keep
it lost a roar over shell sand to zip it
in the mind's eye stalkless and invented
to peer out of places. Gaze steady
across the field, flax in flower as
witness some sprig character burdock
lens for a missed wave, mollify the
flinty surface ordeal over paper, over
what's buried in case of rain not forecast,
over the not known. A service tree as
a surprise by the field margin. The owl
in my heart flies like the hole in my art,
bent blunt by hedgerow, lunette relief
filling memory with its borrowed arch.

All Mere Use

Exiled from the top box viewed from the edge of
some lakeside ground it misled grim supporters no
longer accidental shadows marching along the way.

At least he said it in a language where home was a time
of day or a return ticket, crossing the border as it does
to settle outside any event or thought quite recklessly

adjusting is true of fronts anyway, apostate worries
to sleep on weld or frown over musk mallow light dream
tread. Where will you put yourself when night will fall?

A value circuit then. Quite useful and extensive from day
to day it falls short or we do move beyond the scope
of the view which they say will be gone before flowering.

Wilding Paper

Another bee out of sorts on the foxglove
on the way to peace after tea with all that
bent for chicanery filling every crevice untold
unfolding a thing twice bales of hay today

argued against marginal use or glued new
mulberry chromosome failure overhead
for a rainy day brink to skate on the surface
secretly rating a foundation for military harm

considered account settled as grave dispatch
real figures even poets might flinch at the desert
air suddenly in every issue shaped migration
before brush touches paper, the breath of bark

itself put to invisible use in violent ink
poppy scatter already done so by the log in
time they are fledged and lodge elsewhere
chaffinches and suchlike with their own ethics.

Imported Raw

Part of the conversation against it those branches could be
learnt when they would have his hands over the sun out of the
window flat and wide weighing like the sky imagined in empty
talk for a time, still asleep or half awake and exposed to drive
away how they would be, glint lost in the mist. Reason copied
out in mutual aid before prohibited sweet thought, all they wanted
dropping like flies, liberated unease to proliferate an action *fixe*
often at a true found output traded off and attacked into safer
years later in the century maybe. Dressed up at all levels, dew
so small a distraction agency with a view device hosted by door
frame lighting, all visible to forget their slow emergence to
forge immersion in landscape deceit with dull nightingales—
isn't it great? Smoother paper display clusters coming into flower
as raw material as silence rolls and rolls on as long as it takes.

Acknowledgements

HOME JAMES: 5 poems from the sequence were published as Vol. 1 No. 44 of the Earthbound Poetry Series (2 November 2020)

A SPACE BASED ON HEARSAY was first published in *Black Box Manifold* 25:

http://www.manifold.group.shef.ac.uk/issue25/index25.html

TO ACCOUNT FOR was first published by Face Press (Cambridge, 2021)

IMAGINARY SKY was first published in SNOW *lit rev* 10 (Spring 2022), edited by Anthony Barnett and Ian Brinton.

My thanks to Ian Heames, Alex Houen, Adam Piette, Anthony Barnett and Ian Brinton

LAY OUT YOUR UNREST

Lightning Source UK Ltd.
Milton Keynes UK
UKHW011019050123
414878UK00004B/176

9 781915 079596